God Place

A Walk to Faith

Faith

Love

Poetry
From
The
Heart

Peace

Joy

-- Inspirational and Motivational Poetry --
Poetry From The Heart Collection
By C. Melita Webb

Encouraging, loving and motivational sentiments

ISBN-13: 978-1539816591
ISBN-10: 1539816591

Content Editors: Ruth B. Hill and Emogene Price
Copy Editor: Todd Larson

Cover design: SelfPubBookCovers.com/Daniela
Chapter art: openclipart.org and pixaby.com

Dedication

This book is dedicated to my family, those who are here, those who have passed, and those whom the future will bring my way. Just as you are, is how you were created to be. Your heart remains an inspiration to me. Your life brings more meaning to mine daily. Some of my most inspired moments come from the blessing you are to my life and the joy you are to my soul.

You remain my daily inspiration. Never doubt your importance to me or to this world. The light that shines brightest in my life often comes from you! You are remarkable, and you allow me to believe in a better humanity. Together, we can touch the world and make a difference.

I also dedicate this book to anyone experiencing trials and momentary setbacks. These are some of the words I listen to daily that lift my spirits, allow me to smile, and encourage me to keep moving forward in my life. I am hoping that these words will lift your spirits and help you find a way to make a difference, too.

Foreword

How can two people who have never seen each other be so close. I 'met' Cassandra as I was researching my genealogy and found my cousin. From the first time we spoke our hearts and souls synched. She told me of her passion for writing, how she writes and more importantly....... WHY SHE WRITES. When I read her first book of poetry I was blown away by her insight not only of her life but mine. The way her words flow gives peace and clarity. Most importantly, you know that you are not alone. Each of her books uniquely touches a place in my heart as I know it will in yours. You will be encouraged and more importantly hopeful. Sit back with a cup of tea, coffee or a glass of wine and be blessed/energized by the writings of my cousin Cassie.

Have a Blessed and Positive Day,
Dr. Bonita F. Jones

A Special Thought to the Reader

We serve a loving, faithful God. As the beloved children of a mighty and awesome God, we remain covered by His love, His grace, His protection, and His promise.

My goal for sharing my thoughts is to help us all move to a better place in our lives. As I write what is in my heart and answer friends' questions, I find that everything we want is already present. We just have to be ready to understand who we are and be open to what our spirit is revealing to us.

We must let go of everything holding us back from reaching our dreams and living a happier life. We must work to improve our emotional health, by releasing all hurt, anger, guilt and shame. To truly enjoy life, we must give ourselves the gifts of peace, love, and understanding. We need to let God work in our life and to meet Him with our whole heart.

Keep your spirits high
And your heart full of joy.

Introduction

This book is volume three of the Poetry from the Heart collection. It is designed to provide daily moments of peaceful reflection and to lift your heart and soul higher. It is a wonderful edition to our collection. Included are inspirational poetry, prayers, reflective essays, and motivational prose.

The collection's goals are:

1. To assist readers in recognizing the fullness of their spirit.

2. To support readers in acknowledging their worth and inner beauty.

3. To provide bridges to recognize the depth of their faith, strength and courage.

Our collection is beneficial for all readers—young, old, male, female, happy, sad—as well as readers seeking inspiration who may be in-between understanding their emotions.

Please enjoy the loving journey we have prepared for you.

Table of Contents

Continued

Chapter 2: Faith, Courage and Blessings

Recognizing who we are and what we mean to our Creator. Chapter sentiments focus: Celebrating the gifts and blessings we receive each day.

Poems:
Trusting the Process
Make Life Work
Remain Calm

Essay of Thought: Clearing Our Paths

Chapter 3: Love, Happiness and Peace

Embracing who we are and enjoying life. Chapter sentiments focus: love, joy, happiness and peace.

Prayer: Make Me Over

Poems:
Moving Forward
Release and Embrace
Find the Joy of God

Table of Contents continued

Essay of Thought: Choose to Be Happy

A Note to the Next Generation

Poems:

Essays of Thought:

Closing Prayer: Thank You for Rescuing Me

About the Author

Opening Prayer

Together Through All My Storms

Father,
I thank you for holding me,
For lifting me up
And carrying me through my pain.
For dusting me off,
Polishing my edges,
Caring for my soul
And redefining me in your light.
For standing me back up on my feet.
For reminding me of my worth,
In your eyes.
For seeing me through
My darkest nights.
For holding my mind
And never letting go,
Even when I thought
It was lost to the enemy.

Father, I thank you, for just being you!
My redeemer, my healer,
My counselor and my confidant.

Chapter 1
Welcoming the Day

Let your spirit always remain
In the light of God.

Let the light of your faith
Be a blessing to all those you meet.

**As we open Chapter 1,
ask yourself these three questions:**

1. What does a joyful life look like?

2. What do I want more than anything else, in my joyful life?

3. What must I do to make my life better, to live happier, and to fulfill my dreams?

No matter your answers, always remember:

You were created on purpose.
You are loved.
You are needed.
You are wanted.
You are God's version of love.
He has a plan for your life.

God loves you!

Essay of Thought: Choosing Our Path

We choose most of our life experiences. Yet many of us are still living unhappy lives. Often we do not recognize our strengths or the power we have to make our lives better. When we realize the power of our thoughts, choices and actions, we can begin creating the life we truly want.

It is not too late to change your life for the better. The key is to focus on your faith to see past today's storms. Remember, you are the child of the Most High God, and you never walk alone.

By being more aware of our feelings, needs and desires, we can enact measurable life changes to ensure our happiness. One of the first and best ways to take back your power is to choose to spend your time with people you enjoy being around. People who support you in your dreams, in life, and in love. Making conscious, purposeful choices to bring only good into your personal space will be refreshing, liberating, and downright joyful.

Call into your life the belief that all is well. Breathe deep, say a prayer, and focus on positivity.

Reclaim Your Place

What is that hiding
In your eye?
And on your face?
In your silent sigh?
In your downward gaze?
Tears and shame?
Shame
Does not belong
On your face.
You are a survivor.
Stand tall,
Stand proud,
And reclaim your place.
Remove that sad, sad
Look from your face.
The world,
Our world is better,
Because you are still here.
Because you still live
And you still breathe.
Release your sadness
And embrace
Your rightful place.

God is good and He is always able.
Enjoy what He has prepared for you.

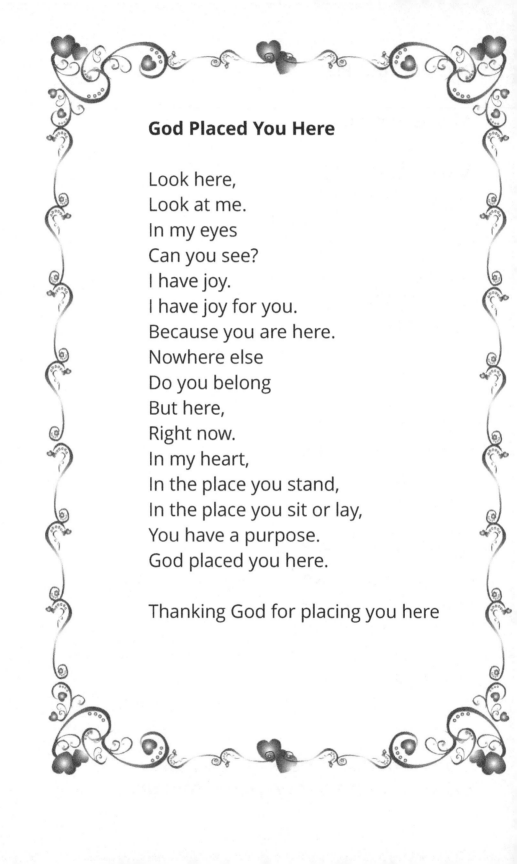

God Placed You Here

Look here,
Look at me.
In my eyes
Can you see?
I have joy.
I have joy for you.
Because you are here.
Nowhere else
Do you belong
But here,
Right now.
In my heart,
In the place you stand,
In the place you sit or lay,
You have a purpose.
God placed you here.

Thanking God for placing you here

You Were Born for Greatness

Blessings were
Spoken for you.
Prayers were written
In our hearts.
Songs were created
And gracefully performed.
Dancers leapt, twirled,
And their spins
Were meticulously executed.
Dreams were renewed,
Hope elevated
And wishes perfected.
Faith in the universe
Was revived.
For me,
The world had once again
Found a key to unlocking
All of life's treasures.
Mountains were moved.
Seas were crossed.
Skies opened
And sacred blessings
Were poured out.
All on the day you were born.
For You Were Born for Greatness.

Believe in a Better Tomorrow

Continue to persevere
Through your trials,
Through your struggles
And through your pains.
Keep going
Until you break through
Whatever is blocking
The clarity you seek,
The dream you desire,
Or the path
You need to take.
Never be afraid
To reach for your dreams.
Choose to allow
Joy to live in your heart.
Always trust, know
And believe,
There is a better tomorrow.

LIFE

Life is today.
Not yesterday,
Nor last week
Or last month.
Life is right now,
With the sweetest dreams
For the future,
With the biggest hopes
For tomorrow.
Life is your present,
Not what happened
In your past.

Focus on your today.
Look for new joys
And new happiness.
Find new meaning
In your today.
Enjoy your current
Precious moment.
Your time,
Your day,
Your right now.
Your life.

Essay of Thought:
Invitation to Positivity

I invite you to speak into your life the blessings you want to receive. You can create the life you want by releasing everything preventing you from reaching your inner peace and your divine destiny.

Bring into your focus only thoughts of a peaceful, joyful life. Clear your mind of every troubling thought. Refresh and renew your soul with God's word.

Choose to be happier, and choose to be free from all stress and all negativity. Release all that God has called you to release. Release everything of no benefit to your soul's well-being.

Never forget—you are God's beloved creation. He took time to awaken your soul and to breathe air into your lungs. He caressed your newborn body and comforted you as you entered this world. With His love, you are worthy, and you are complete.

Continued

God does not desire his beloved children to live under difficult conditions. You can find your way to peace. Always remember, you have His support and He has you wrapped in His arms, and He is holding you tight. Trust and believe— God will never let you go.

You are His beloved creation.

We are all children
Of His promise.
His promise lives in me,
And His promise lives in you.
Therefore, peace will always
Be the answer
For how we move forward.

Blessed child of God,
Keep shining your light and
Sharing your beautiful and loving spirit.
Your presence brightens the world.
Know that all will be well.

Unique child of God,
Accept yourself
For the blessing that you are.
God placed you here with a purpose.
Be open to new possibilities.
You are only limited,
By your choices, dreams and beliefs.

Compassionate child of God,
Continue to be at peace.
Enjoy the new day with a smile.
Be thankful for another day
To live, to learn, to love and to grow.
Goodness is coming your way.

Faithful child of God,
Start today with fresh new eyes.
Focus only on peace and positivity.
Have faith in everything you do.
Realize your challenges
Will bring you deeper understanding.

Triumphant child of God,
Do not get lost in yesterday's struggle.
Rejoice for each new day is a blessing-
A new chance to be happier,
And to be more present in your life.
Choose to live your life renewed.
Look for new opportunities.

Courageous child of God,
Welcome the new day
With a fresh new attitude.
Release all your hurt, any anger,
All your fears and uncried tears.
Make today, the day you desire.
Choose your own destiny and
Act to create your own fate.

Accomplished child of God,
Keep an open heart.
Allow nothing to block your kind spirit.
Free your heart and mind of all worries.
Focus only on: new hopes, new dreams
And new aspirations.
You are who God created you to be.

Gracious child of God,
Your are a much-needed light
In this world.
You are strong, courageous,
And effective at what you do.
Be proud, be bold
And be comfortable being you.

Joyful child of God,
Smile and keep your faith.
Let nothing deter you
From living a joyful life.
Continue believing in all that is good.
As you go through your day,
Know that something wonderful
Is coming your way.

Peaceful child of God,
Start today with calming thoughts.
Release all anger, stress, worry and fear.
God has already prepared you
With what you need to succeed.
Acknowledge that you are capable
Of reaching your dreams.
Trust, know and believe,
God has put into motion
The changes we need for peace.

Beloved child of God,
Each new day
Is a morning kiss from God.
A blessing and a new beginning.
You must have faith
And you must believe,
To manifest your dreams
Into your reality.
Create a day that brings you only
Love, joy, happiness and peace.

Honored child of God,
Everyday you are alive,
Will always be special.
When you wake and see a new day,
Smile and enjoy
The blessing it is to be alive.
Call into your life: love,
Calm, serenity and peace.

Virtuous child of God,
Rejoice in the new day.
Your heartfelt prayers were heard.
Your toughest battles have
Already been won.
Continue to stay focused and
Lean on His word for guidance.

Beautiful child of God,
Never give up.
Know that our Father
Is always surrounding you
With His love, His power
And His spirit.
God's strength is all you need.
He will always carry you through.

Loving child of God,
Keep going to meet your goals
And to live your best life.
Keep moving forward
And keep growing in your faith.
Continue to look for positivity.
Do not stop now.
You are a champion.

Determined child of God,
You are not defeated.
Never let anything hold you down.
Do not let fear
Keep you in it's embrace.
You are never alone.
There is no place you can travel
Where God is not found.
God is always with you.

Chapter 2
Faith, Courage and Blessings

You are always worthy.

You are a remarkable creation,
a testimony of God's eternal love.

As we open Chapter 2, bring into your focus thoughts of peace, strength and courage.

Remain Calm

Blessed child of God,
Maintain peace in your heart.
Remain calm in your mind,
And stay in control
Of your feelings.
Do everything you can
To be peaceful
And to live in harmony.
Your life is important.
We need you to live.
We need you to love.
We need you to survive,
To thrive,
And to continue to stand.
The only way your life
Makes a difference, is if you live.

God placed you here.

Trusting the Process

Trusting,
That we all have a purpose.
Knowing,
God placed us here.
Living,
Through our precious moments,
Of time, of life,
And sometimes,
Living with daily challenges.
We keep moving.
Through the years,
Through the occasional fears
And undefined tears.
Reaching up,
Out of the darkness.
To comeback,
Stand and try again.
We continue to fight
And to rise like a Phoenix.
We, when we are united,
Will always be able to stand.
We are all God's people.

Make Life Work

You my dear
Are a fabulous child of God.
You can
And you will,
Have a marvelous day.
Start it over,
Right now
With a deep breath.
Focus only on happy memories
And remember to smile.
Make today go your way.
You are one special child of God.
No one can do you,
Better than you.
Shake it off.
Make today work,
And make your life work.

Clearing Our Paths

Sometimes we do not recognize the path we are walking on. I believe this is because we are not the only ones on that path. God is there with us. We do not see Him, but the five senses He gives us are always with us. In addition, we have our intuition that helps guide us.

Sometimes we get into trouble, because we think we are on the path alone. We ignore our inner wisdom and our intuition. Other times we do not think about the gifts and blessings that are all around us. We do not think of the roadblocks as ways to grow. More often, we think of them as proof that life has to be hard. Usually, we do not understand that the blocks are put there to help us learn to make better decisions on the rest of the path.

Sometimes the roadblock comes in the form of an illness, an injury, someone walking into or out of your life unexpectedly, and other trials you do not see for what they are. But they are all things designed to help us grow into who we are supposed to be.

Continued

Some people have roadblocks they are never able to get through. They appear locked in an unhappy, unproductive and sometimes continuing sad state of existence. Others seem to kick roadblocks out of their way and pretend they were never there in the first place. A third set of people finds ways to push the roadblock away, move it around, or climb over it. If you take any of these three roads, you will repeat the pattern that brought you to the roadblock in the first place.

To remove the challenges, you must deal with the issue or issues. Choose to resolve your challenges as they occur so you will have a clearer path tomorrow.

Be strong and be courageous.
For God is always with us.
—Joshua 1:9

Victorious child of God,
Rejoice for God is your support,
Your rock and your redeemer.
See with fresh eyes,
Take in all of God's beauty.
Expect greatness,
For nothing else awaits you.

Protected child of God,
See through eyes of love.
Be thankful and recognize
The beauty all around you.
Listen with your heart
And hear the beauty of your soul.
You are well loved, highly favored,
And your future is bright.

Empowered child of God,
Work through your challenges.
Know that when you break through,
Understanding and peace await you.
Your challenges are a part of
What gives you strength,
Compassion, and empathy.

Favored child of God,
Always remember,
There is a place in this world
Where you fit in perfectly.
Be true to yourself.
Acknowledge your strengths
And seek to understand
Your challenges.

Gifted child of God,
Your are a beacon of light
And a blessed ray of hope.
Continue to let your light shine.
Live by faith
And walk in your truth.
You are the prize, the gift,
And you are full of promise.

Cherished child of God,
Realize you are capable
Of reaching all your dreams.
God prepared you at birth
With the knowledge you need.
Dig down deep and believe,
You are already equipped
With what is necessary
For you to succeed.

Wonderful child of God,
You are always worthy.
You are a daily blessing to all
Who know and love you.
Believe in yourself
And in all your strengths.
Never again doubt
What you are able to achieve!

Remarkable child of God,
You are blessed beyond measure.
The full magnitude of the talents,
Gifts and blessings
God has bestowed upon you
Is yet to be realized.
Remain open to receive new blessings,
The universe is sending your way.

Honored child of God,
You are only scratching
The surface of your worth.
You have so much power in your
Heart, mind, body and soul.
Know and believe,
You can define your own day.
You have the power
To create a better life.

Dedicated child of God,
Rest assured you are deeply loved.
God knows the content of your heart
And He will never abandon you.
He continues to cover you
With His love and His grace.
Remember His word
And keep a smile on your face.

Wise child of God,
Remove the stress from your chest.
You can and will find your joy.
You will survive every storm.
God remains with you.
Keep smiling and remember,
Your best days are yet to come.

Rejoicing child of God,
You are a natural born winner.
You were created to succeed.
Remain encouraged in all that you do.
Stay in your faith and allow
God to be your guide.
God is in control
And He always has a master plan.
Smile, and be at peace.

Redeemed child of God,
Release your past
And all bad memories.
Forgive yourself, and love yourself
Through the old pain.
Then move forward in your life.
Start today renewed, refreshed,
And committed to being a better you.
Choose to see,
The blessings all around you.

Treasured child of God,
Never question your purpose
Or your existence.
You are perfect, in your imperfection.
Keep walking your path with pride.
Embrace your faith and know,
God is always by your side.

Trusting child of God,
Live graciously in your faith.
Embrace your courage.
God's strength,
Will always sustain you,
As you are covered
In God's unfailing love
And His unwavering affection.

Powerful child of God,
You are beautiful,
And a much-needed light in this world.
You are strong
And effective at what you do.
Be proud, be bold,
And be comfortable being you.

Chapter 3
Love, Happiness and Peace

Keep your joy and stay in peace.
God is in control,
And His justice will prevail.

Embrace your passion for life
And believe in who you are.

God's words will always encourage you
And be a bridge to a more peaceful life.

Prayer : Make Me Over

Father,
Make me over
So there is no more anger
Left in my emotion.
So there is no more pain
Left in my memory.
So that my very soul sings
Songs of Your sweet love.
So that all I speak
Is Your peaceful word.
So that with every step I take,
I glorify and praise Your name.
Father, please
Touch me
And make me over.

*As we open Chapter 3,
bring into your focus thoughts of
faith, love and happiness*

Moving Forward

How do we move forward
When we cannot see?
We must have faith,
And we must believe.
Focus on your end goals.
Pray about what you need.
Visualize your path
And then proceed.
Make some time today,
To start living your dreams.

God loves you!

Release and Embrace

Sweet child of God,
Who lives perfectly
In His loving Embrace,
Release all of your worries,
And Embrace your joy.
Call into your life
All of God's blessings.
Call into your space
Only positivity.
Call into your world
An abundance of love
While you enjoy
The glory of God
And all of His grace.
God's grace
Is always sufficient
To see you through.

Find the Joy of God

Find the joy of God
That lives in your heart,
That fuels your being,
That lifts your head
On your most tired days.

Live in the joy of God
That brings comfort
In your darkest hours,
That continues to lead you
To remain in your faith.

That is the joy of God
That you must cling to everyday.

Essay of Thought: Choose to Be Happy

Not everyone you have in your life means you well. Some of those we love—family, friends, coworkers, neighbors, acquaintances—are mean, spiteful, angry, hurt, or jealous. You do not have to do anything for others to rejoice in your challenges. They may not even realize that they are bringing negativity to you.

If you have people in your life that bring out the worst in you, keep you unhappy, or make you feel unloved, uncared for or less than your worth when they are around, they are "spirit blockers." Their mere presence can reduce your joy and your positivity. They can block those blessings you do not even see coming.

It is hard to let loved ones go. I promise you, it is more difficult, and can be devastating, to allow them to remain a constant in your life.

Continued

Only you can decide that you have had enough poor treatment, bad interactions and blocked happiness. Only you can decide that you want better for yourself, that you are worth more than the negative energy they cause when they block your positivity. Only you can decide to say 'Yes' to a better life for yourself.

Not everyone will want you to excel, improve the quality of your life, or live happily. Some do not expect or want more for themselves. So why would you expect them to want more for you?

My suggestion is to move away from unhappiness. Move yourself and your household to a place of joy and peace. You can invite others to join you on your quest for peace and tranquility. It is, however, up to them to join you. If they still choose negativity, you have a different choice to make. They may not belong in your inner circle of friends and family.

The best gift you can give yourself is to surround yourself with people who love and cherish you as much as you love and cherish them.

Priceless child of God,
See yourself being
All that God created you to be.
Never forget your worth.
You are His masterpiece.
You are one of God's finest creations.
You are His priceless, irreplaceable
Work of art.

Giving child of God,
Love and support yourself,
As you love and support others.
Put all your energy into peace.
Peace must remain your focus.
Giving yourself the gift of peace
Is one way to show yourself love.

Brave child of God,
Trust your intuition.
Your spirit knows what you need.
Remain prepared to achieve.
There is more strength in you
Than you believe.
Keep looking higher, thinking deeper
And becoming more
Of who you are meant to be.

Precious child of God,
Your life has a special meaning,
And you have a divine purpose.
Seek to be the light
You were created to be.
Rise and walk into your greatness.
You will always
Be needed in this world.

Peaceful Child of God,
Always believe
In the champion inside of you.
Stay strong and breathe deep.
Wear a smile and step out on faith.
You are powerful, creative, intelligent,
And you are enough.

Enlightened child of God,
Stay in your faith and never give up.
Even when things look bleak
And you can not see your way through,
Remain deep in your faith.
God will see for you.
God will hear for you,
And He will stand for you.
God is all you ever need.

Intelligent child of God
Seek to find balance in your life
And to reside in your inner peace.
Take the time and steps necessary
To lovingly support yourself
Emotionally, physically, and spiritually.
Keep love in your heart
And God's word on your mind.

Creative child of God,
Focus on what gives you peace.
Surround yourself with love.
Choose to make your life better,
Live your life fuller
And choose to love yourself more.
Only place your cares, thoughts
And energy where they are valued,
Appreciated and needed.

Talented child of God,
Continue to share your love
And your knowledge.
You never know who's heart
You are meant to touch,
Or who you will help succeed.

Forgiven child of God,
Listen to your heart
To find the answers you need most.
Often, the most beneficial answers
Come from deep within.
Choose to see your life
Through the eyes of God's love.

A note to the Next Generation:
Inspired by my Children and Grandchildren

My greatest life moments
Have been shared with you.
Envisioning your daily moments
When you are not with me.
Wondering which new joys
You have discovered today.
Remembering the first time
I saw your precious face
And held you near.
Laughing at the way you wobbled
When you took your first steps.
Shaking my head
At how no one who loves you
Can tell you "no" to anything.
Rejoicing in the memories
Of the greatest gift ever given to me:
That gift is you.
Learning to love the little things
And seeing the world
Through your beautiful eyes.
Listening to the wonderment,
Discovery, joy,
And amazement in your voice.
Discovering miracles in your face,
Listening to your heart
And feeling your precious touch.
Who knew, I could love anyone this much?

Keep Going

Continue to persevere
Through your trials,
Through your struggles,
And through your pains.
Keep going
Until you break through
Whatever is blocking
The clarity you seek,
The dream you desire
Or the path you need to take.
Never be afraid
To reach for your dreams.
Always trust, know
And believe,
There is a better tomorrow.

God Has A Plan

Sometimes
Seasons of life's journey
Are like a bad dream.
You may feel trapped,
And you may feel alone.
You are not.
God is always with you.
You may not understand
Or even know what you need.
God knows your circumstances,
And He has a plan.
He will help you find
The calm, peace, love
And the joy you seek.

Poem of Encouragement

Beautiful child of God,
Keep shining your light bright.
Continue being a reflection
Of all that is good.
Never give up!
Know that you are a miracle.
Your life is important.
No matter what
You are going through,
You are equipped
To handle all your challenges.
God has already said so.
You have unrealized power,
Strength and wisdom.
You will always achieve
For God's blessing is upon you.

Essay of Thought : Life's Challenges

Unexpected changes in life are like roadblocks. We must take the time to work through the detour to get to the other side.

Sometimes these changes or roadblocks appear to directly challenge us. We must recognize that challenges drive us to become more of who we are meant to be. We must meet the difficulties and master the lessons necessary to learn and grow.

Once you go through the challenge, deal with the change, or resolve the roadblock, your future awaits.

Pray and stay in your deepest faith. You will find the way past your fears.

Your future awaits!

Essay of Thought: Struggles and Faith

I am convinced that not every test or struggle is a test of faith. Sometimes it is a test of will, like, will you make a decision to do what needs to be done?

Other times it is a test of your personal choice, your desire to enact change in your own life— for example, to find lost keys, to get a job done, to decide to get up and get moving. Sometimes we just lack energy, enthusiasm or motivation. That is not a lack of faith.

Learning what is important is a test of the mind. You can make poor choices all day, but many are not tests of faith, just test of senses, common sense, book-sense, and your desire to uphold community obligations.

So when you are tested, look deeper at the test. Not everything is about your faith—many times it is just about you.

Closing Prayer:

Thank You For Rescuing Me

Thank you, God,
For continuing to love me,
For continuously guiding me,
My mind and my choices.
Thank you for
Removing the negativity
That was around me,
For clearing the path
That now lies before me,
For destroying
The stumbling blocks
That would prevent me
From living more freely
In your word.
Thank you
For rescuing me,
And for showing me
I am worthy.

About the Author

C. Melita Webb is a lover of life, who is visually challenged. She has loved words and books all her life. As a student, she excelled in writing deeply touching and reflective prose. Publishing was a dream she gave up on 30+ years ago, though she continued to write in her heart, mind and spirit. Later, she began speaking and writing into the hearts of her family and friends, too.

In fact, it was at the request of a loved one that the first book was published. She had no idea how powerful her words would still be, or how many had longed to find a voice like hers.

Her writings are full of passion, clarity and purpose. They span many years and phases of life. Each book in her collection tells a story of love, life, and humanity. Included are reflective poems, loving affirmations, supportive prayers, motivational essays, and cries from the heart. She writes the words that live in all our hearts.

God Placed You Here is a perfect gift for you, or someone you care for. Please enjoy this collection with our love and best wishes.

— The Poetry From the Heart team

**Other Poetry From the Heart books
by C. Melita Webb**

Book one in Poetry From the Heart Collection:
All is Redeemed in Truth and Light,
Kindle Edition, ASIN: B01I8RTZCK,
July 2016
ISBN-13: 978-1535329989
ISBN-10: 15353299X

Book two in Poetry From the Heart Collection:
The Light That is You
Kindle Edition, ASIN: B01M72UNGO,
October 2016
ISBN-13: 978-1537781358
ISBN-10: 1537781359

Please visit us at www.cmelitawebb.com

Made in United States
Orlando, FL
05 August 2024

49963294R00050